Old English Nursery Songs

Old·English Nursery Songs

Uniform with this Volume

OLD FRENCH NURSERY SONGS

Thirty Traditional Nursery Songs. Arranged and Illustrated by ANNE ANDERSON. With Eight Plates in Colours and many Line Drawings and Decorations.

THE SLEEPY SONG BOOK

Containing Twelve Songs by EUGENE FIELD, MAY BYRON, and F. CAMPBELL, set to Music by H. A. J. CAMPBELL. With Twelve Plates in Colours and Decorations in Line by ANNE ANDERSON.

Old English Nursery Songs

Music Arranged by
Horace Mansion

Pictured by
Anne Anderson

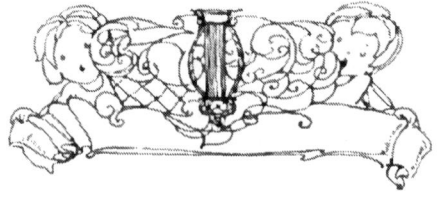

London · George G. Harrap & Co Ltd
And at Sydney

979.879

		PAGE
I.	Oranges and Lemons	9
II.	Hey, Diddle, Diddle	12
III.	Little Bo-peep	14
IV.	Hush-a-bye, Baby	16
V.	Twinkle, Twinkle, Little Star	19
VI.	Humpty Dumpty	22
VII.	Jack and Jill	24
VIII.	See-saw, Marjory Daw	26
IX.	Goosey, Goosey, Gander	28
X.	What Are Little Boys Made Of?	29
XI.	Ride a Cock-horse	32
XII.	Sing a Song of Sixpence	35
XIII.	Hickory, Dickory, Dock	36
XIV.	Baa, Baa, Black Sheep	38
XV.	Tom, Tom, the Piper's Son	40
XVI.	Here We Go Round the Mulberry Bush	41
XVII.	Curly Locks	44
XVIII.	Mistress Mary, Quite Contrary	47
XIX.	Old King Cole	48
XX.	Pussy Cat, Pussy Cat	50
XXI.	Sleep, Baby, Sleep	52
XXII.	Three Children Sliding	54

CONTENTS—Continued

		PAGE
XXIII.	BABY BUNTING	56
XXIV.	LITTLE JACK HORNER	59
XXV.	THE CARRION CROW	60
XXVI.	PAT-A-CAKE	62
XXVII.	SIMPLE SIMON	64
XXVIII.	RUB-A-DUB, DUB	66
XXIX.	THREE BLIND MICE	69
XXX.	LONDON BRIDGE	70
XXXI.	COME, FOLLOW ME	72
XXXII.	GIRLS AND BOYS	74
XXXIII.	I SAW THREE SHIPS	76
XXXIV.	GOOD KING WENCESLAS	79
XXXV.	THE FIRST NOËL	82
XXXVI.	DING, DONG, BELL	84
XXXVII.	WHERE ARE YOU GOING TO, MY PRETTY MAID?	86

1

" Oranges and Lemons," say the bells of Saint Clement's.
" You owe me five farthings," say the bells of Saint Martin's.
" When will you pay me ? " say the bells of Old Bailey.
" When I get rich," say the bells of Shoreditch.

    Ding dong, ding ding dong,
    Ding dong, ding ding dong.

2

" When will that be ? " say the bells of Stepney.
" I do not know," says the great bell of Bow.
" Pancakes and fritters," say the bells of Saint Peter's.
" Two sticks and an apple," say the bells of Whitechapel.

    Ding dong, etc.

3

" Old father Bald-pate," say the slow bells of Aldgate.
" Pokers and tongs," say the bells of Saint John's.
" Kettles and pans," say the bells of Saint Anne's.
" Brickbats and tiles," say the bells of Saint Giles.

    Ding dong, etc.

Little Bo-peep
Has lost her sheep,
And doesn't know where to find them.
Leave them alone,
And they'll come home,
And bring their tails behind them.

Little Bo-peep
Fell fast asleep,
And dreamt she heard them bleating ;
But when she awoke,
She found it a joke,
For still they all were fleeting ;

Then up she took
Her little crook,
Determined for to find them ;
She found them indeed,
But it made her heart bleed,
For they'd left their tails behind them.

It happened one day,
As Bo-peep did stray
Unto a meadow hard by,
There she espied
Their tails side by side,
All hung on a tree to dry.

TWINKLE, TWINKLE, LITTLE STAR

1

Twinkle, twinkle, little star,
How I wonder what you are,
Up above the world so high,
Like a diamond in the sky.

    Twinkle, twinkle, little star,
    How I wonder what you are.

2

When the blazing sun is gone,
When he nothing shines upon,
Then you show your little light,
Twinkle, twinkle, all the night.

    Twinkle, twinkle, etc.

3

Then the traveller in the dark
Thanks you for your tiny spark.
Could he see which way to go
If you did not twinkle so?

    Twinkle, twinkle, etc.

4

In the dark blue sky you keep
While you through my curtains peep,
And you never shut your eye
Till the sun is in the sky.

    Twinkle, twinkle, etc.

HUMPTY DUMPTY

Hump-ty Dump-ty sat on a wall, Hump-ty Dump-ty had a great fall; All the King's hor-ses and all the King's men Could-n't set up Hump-ty Dump-ty a-gain.

Song VII. Jack and Jill

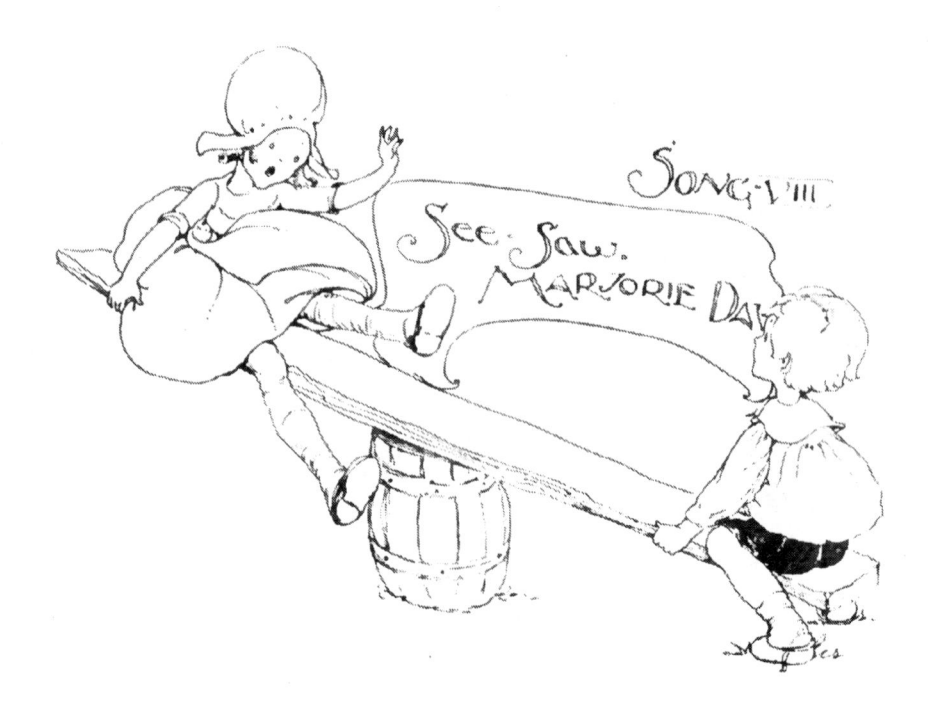

Song VIII. See-Saw, Marjorie Daw

JACK AND JILL

1. Jack and Jill went up the hill To fetch a pail of water; Jack fell down and broke his crown, And Jill came tumbling af-ter. 2. Then

JACK & JILL

1

Jack and Jill went up the hill
    To fetch a pail of water,
Jack fell down and broke his crown,
    And Jill came tumbling after.

2

Then up Jack got and home did trot,
    As fast as he could caper;
Dame Jill had the job to plaster his nob
    With vinegar and brown paper.

3

Jill came in, and she did grin
    To see his paper plaster;
Her mother, vexed, did whip her next
    For laughing at Jack's disaster.

4

This made Jill pout, and she ran out,
    And Jack did quickly follow;
They rode dog Ball, till Jill did fall,
    Which made Jack laugh and hollo.

SEE-SAW-MARJORIE-DAW

See-saw, Mar-jo-ry Daw, Har-ry shall have a new mas-ter; He shall have but a pen-ny a day, Be-cause he won't work an-y fast-er.

Song IX
GOOSEY, GOOSEY GANDER.

Song X.
WHAT are LITTLE BOYS made of?

RIDE-A-COCK-HORSE.
Song XI

Goosey-Goosey Gander

Goo-sey, goo-sey, gan-der, Whi-ther shall I wan-der?
Up-stairs and down-stairs, And in my la-dy's cham-ber.
There I met an old man, who would not say his pray'rs, I took him by the left leg, And threw him down the stairs.

WHAT are LITTLE BOYS MADE OF?

1. What are lit-tle boys made of? What are lit-tle boys made of? Frogs and snails and lit-tle dog's tails, And that are lit-tle boys made of.

2. What are lit-tle girls made of? What are lit-tle girls made of? Su-gar and spice and all that's nice And that are lit-tle girls made of.

WHAT ARE LITTLE BOYS MADE OF?

1

What are little boys made of?
What are little boys made of?
Frogs and snails and little dog's tails,
And that are little boys made of.

2

What are little girls made of?
What are little girls made of?
Sugar and spice, and all that's nice,
And that are little girls made of.

3

What are young men made of?
What are young men made of?
Sighs and leers and crocodile tears,
And that are young men made of.

4

What are young women made of?
What are young women made of?
Ribbons and laces, and sweet pretty faces,
And that are young women made of.

RIDE-A-COCK HORSE.

Ride a cock-horse to Ban-bur-y Cross, To
see an old la-dy up-on a white horse;
Rings on her fin-gers and bells on her toes,
She shall have mu-sic wher-ev-er she goes.

Song XII
Sing a Song o' Sixpence.

Song XIII
Hickory Dickory Dock

Song XIV
Baa, Baa, Black Sheep.

The King was in his counting house.

SING-A-SONG O' SIXPENCE

1. Sing a song of sixpence, a pocket full of rye,
Four and twenty blackbirds baked in a pie;
When the pie was open'd the birds began to sing,
Wasn't that a dainty dish to set before a king?

2. The King was in his counting-house, counting out his money,
The queen was in the parlour, eating bread and honey,
The maid was in the garden, hanging out the clothes,
There came a little blackbird and peck'd off her nose.

HICKORY-DICKORY DOCK!

Hick-o-ry, dick-o-ry, dock! The mouse ran up the clock, The clock struck one, And down it ran, Hick-o-ry, dick-o-ry, dock!

1

Hickory, dickory, dock !
The mouse ran up the clock,
The clock struck one,
And down it ran,
Hickory, dickory, dock !

2

Hickory, dickory, dock,
The mouse ran up the clock,
The clock struck three,
The mouse ran away,
Hickory, dickory, dock

3

Hickory, dickory, dock,
The mouse ran up the clock,
The clock struck ten,
The mouse came again,
Hickory, dickory, dock.

BAA, BAA BLACK SHEEP

Baa, baa, black sheep, have you an-y wool?
Yes, sir, yes, sir, three bags full. One for the mas-ter,
one for the dame, And one for the lit-tle boy that lives in our lane.

SONG XV.

TOM, TOM, the PIPER'S SON.

SONG XVI.

HERE we go Round the Mulberry Bush.

SONG XVII

CURLY LOCKS!

TOM · TOM ·
THE · PIPER'S · SON.

Tom, Tom, the Pi - per's son,
Stole a pig and a - way did run; The pig was eat and
Tom was beat, Which sent him howl - ing down the street.

Here We Go Round the Mulberry Bush

1. Here we go round the mulberry bush, The mulberry bush, The mulberry bush, Here we go round the mulberry bush, So early in the morning.

2. This is the way we wash our clothes, We
wash our clothes, We wash our clothes, This is the way we
wash our clothes, So ear - ly Mon - day morn - ing.

3

This is the way we iron our clothes, etc.,
So early Tuesday morning.

4

This is the way we scrub the floor, etc.,
So early Wednesday morning.

5

This is the way we mend our clothes, etc.,
So early Thursday morning.

6

This is the way we sweep the house, etc.,
So early Friday morning.

7

This is the way we bake our bread, etc.,
So early Saturday morning.

8

This is the way we go to church, etc.,
So early Sunday morning.

CURLY LOCKS!

Curly locks! curly locks!
Wilt thou be mine? Thou shalt not wash
dishes, Nor yet feed the swine, But
sit on a cushion And
sew a fine seam, And
feed upon strawberries, Sugar and cream.

Song XVIII

MISTRESS MARY

Song XIX

OLD KING COLE

Song XX

Pussy-Cat, Pussy-Cat
Where have you been?

MISTRESS MARY.

Mistress Mary, quite contrary,
How does your garden grow? With silver bells and
cockle shells, And pretty maids all of a row.

OLD KING COLE

1.2. Old King Cole was a mer-ry old soul And a mer-ry old soul was he, And he call'd for his pipe and he call'd for his bowl, And he call'd for his { 1. fid-dlers / 2. har-pers } three. Now

WAS·A·MERRY·OLD·SOUL;
ev' - ry {1. fid-dler / 2. har-per} had a {1. fid - dle / 2. harp so} fine, And a
ver-y fine {1. fid-dle / 2. harp} had he, {1. Twee-dle - dee, twee-dle - dee, / 2. Then twang-a - twang,} went the
{1. fid - dlers / 2. har - pers} three, Old King Cole and his {1. fid - dlers / 2. har - pers} three.

PUSSY-CAT, PUSSY-CAT

Pus-sy cat, pus-sy cat, where have you been? I've been to Lon-don to look at the Queen. Pus-sy cat, pus-sy cat, what did you there? I caught a lit-tle mouse un-der the chair.

Song XXI

Sleep·Baby·Sleep.

Song XXII

Three Children Sliding.

Song XXIII·

Baby·Baby Bunting

SLEEP, BABY, SLEEP

Adagio.

1. Sleep, ba - by, sleep! Thy fa - ther wat-ches the sheep, And tend-eth the lambs up - on yon-der hill, But mo - ther wat-ches one dear-er still, Sleep, ba - by, sleep.

1

 Sleep, baby, sleep!
 Thy father watches the sheep,
And tendeth the lambs upon yonder hill,
But mother watches one dearer still,
 Sleep, baby, sleep!

2

 Sleep, baby, sleep!
 Soft be thy slumbers and deep,
While over our heads wild winds meet,
An old, old lullaby they repeat.
 Sleep, baby, sleep!

3

 Sleep, baby, sleep!
 The baby knows not to weep
Unconscious it lies of the toil of life,
Knows nothing yet of its din and strife,
 Sleep, baby, sleep!

4

 Sleep, baby, sleep!
 Thy father watches the sheep,
And tendeth the lambs upon yonder hill,
But mother watches one dearer still,
 Sleep, baby, sleep!

Three Children Sliding

1. Three children sliding on the ice, All on a summer's day, As it fell out, they all fell in, And the rest they ran away.

1

Three children sliding on the ice,
All on a summer's day,
As it fell out, they all fell in,
And the rest they ran away

2

Now had these children been at home
Or sliding on dry ground,
Ten thousand pounds to one penny,
They had not all been drowned

3

You parents all, that children have,
And you too, that have none,
If you would have them safe abroad,
Pray keep them safe at home.

BABY BABY BUNTING.

Baby baby Bunting,
Daddy's gone a hunting;
Gone to get a rabbit skin,
To wrap the baby Bunting in.

Song XXIV.

Little Jack Horner

Song XXV.

Carrion Crow.

Song XXVI.

Pat-a-cake — Pat-a-cake.

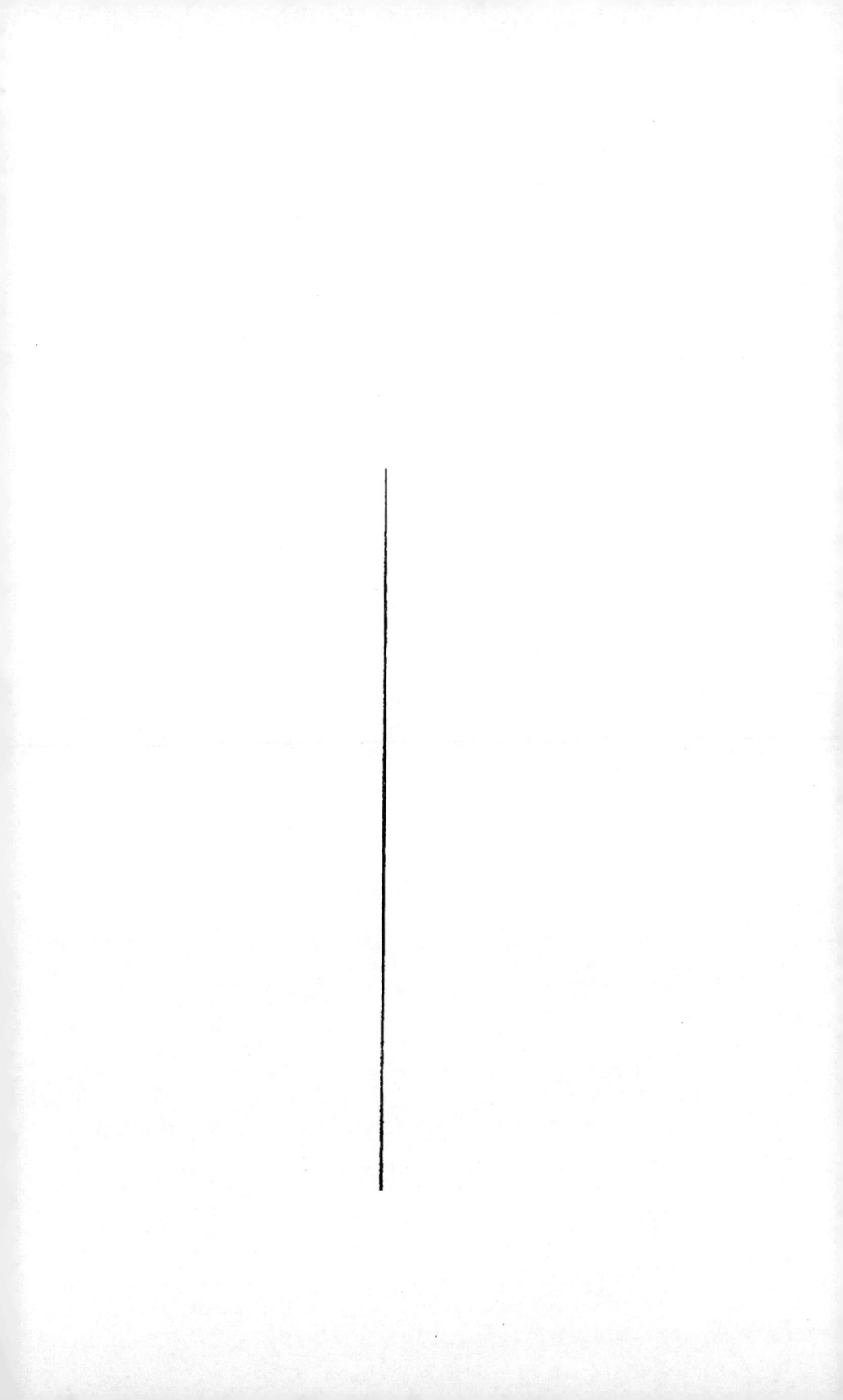

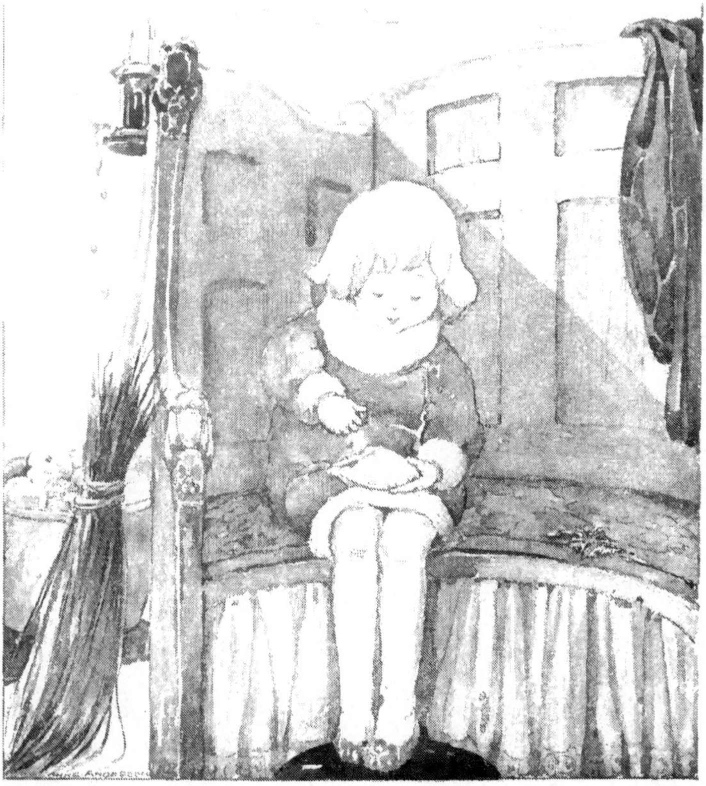

Little Jack Horner

Little Jack Horner sat in a corner,
Eating a Christmas pie;
He put in his thumb, and pull'd out a plum,
And said, "What a good boy am I!"

CARRION CROW

1. A carrion crow sat on an oak, Derry, derry, derry, dee-co; A carrion crow sat on an oak, Watching a tailor shape his cloak, Heigh ho, the carrion crow, Derry, derry, derry, dee-co.

A carrion crow sat on an oak,
Derry, derry, derry, deeco;
A carrion crow sat on an oak,
Watching a tailor shape his coat
    Heigh ho, the carrion crow,
    Derry, derry, derry, deeco

"Oh! wife, bring me my old bent bow,
Derry, derry, derry, deeco,
Oh! wife, bring me my old bent bow,
That I may shoot yon carrion crow"
    Heigh ho, etc

The tailor shot, and missed his mark,
Derry, derry, derry, deeco,
The tailor shot, and missed his mark,
And shot his own sow through the heart
    Heigh ho, etc

"Oh wife! oh wife! some brandy in a spoon,
Derry, derry, derry, deeco,
Oh wife! oh wife! some brandy in a spoon,
For our old sow is in a swoon"
    Heigh ho, etc

The old sow died, and the bells did toll,
Derry, derry, derry, deeco;
The old sow died, and the bells did toll,
And the little pigs prayed for the old sow's soul
    Heigh ho, etc.

Pat-a-Cake- Pat-a-Cake- Baker's-Man

Pat a cake, pat a cake, baker's man,
So I will, master, as fast as I can. Pat it and prick it and
mark it with B, And put it in th' ov-en for Ba-by and me.

SONG XXVII
SIMPLE SIMON

RUB-A-DUB-DUB
SONG XXVIII

Simple Simon

1. Simple Simon met a pieman
Going to the fair. Says Simple Simon
to the pieman: "Let me taste your ware."

1

Simple Simon met a pieman
   Going to the fair.
Says Simple Simon to the pieman ·
   " Let me taste your ware."

2

Says the pieman to Simple Simon
   " Show me first your penny."
Says Simple Simon to the pieman
   " Indeed I have not any."

3

Simple Simon went a-fishing
   For to catch a whale.
But all the water he had got
   Was in his mother's pail

4

Simple Simon went to look
   If plums grew on a thistle.
He pricked his fingers very much
   Which made poor Simon whistle

RUB-A-DUB, DUB

Rub - a - dub, dub, Three men in a tub, Who do you think were there?— The but-cher, the ba-ker, The can-dle-stick ma-ker, And they are all gone to the fair.

Song XXIX

Three-Blind Mice.

Song XXX.

London Bridge is falling down.

Song XXXI.

Come, follow me.

THREE BLIND MICE

LONDON BRIDGE
is falling down.

1. Lon-don Bridge is fall-ing down,
Fall-ing down, fall-ing down, Lon-don Bridge is
fall-ing down, My fair la-dy.

1
London Bridge is falling down,
Falling down, falling down,
London Bridge is falling down,
    My fair lady

2
Build it up with iron bars,
Iron bars, iron bars,
Build it up with iron bars,
    My fair lady

3
Iron bars will bend and break,
Bend and break, bend and break,
Iron bars will bend and break,
    My fair lady

4
Build it up with gold and silver,
Gold and silver, gold and silver,
Build it up with gold and silver,
    My fair lady

5
Build it up with stone so strong,
Stone so strong, stone so strong,
Build it up with stone so strong,
    My fair lady

6
Then 'twill last for ages long,
Ages long, ages long,
Then 'twill last for ages long,
    My fair lady

Come Follow Me

Allegro.

1. Come, fol-low, fol-low, fol-low, fol-low, fol-low, fol-low me.
2. Whi-ther shall I fol-low, fol-low, fol-low, Whi-ther shall I fol-low, fol-low thee?
3. To the green-wood, to the green-wood, to the green-wood, green-wood tree.

Song XXXII

Girls & Boys

Song XXXIII

I saw three Ships

GIRLS AND BOYS

Girls and boys, come out to play, The moon doth shine as bright as day; Leave your sup-per and leave your sleep, And join your play-fel-lows in the street. Come with a whoop!

COME·OUT·TO·PLAY

come with a call! Come with a good will or not at all.

Up the lad-der and down the wall, A half-pen-ny roll will serve us all.

You find milk, and I'll find flour, And we'll have a pud-ding in half an hour.

I SAW THREE SHIPS

1. I saw three ships come sail - ing by,
Sail - ing by, sail - ing by, I saw three ships come sail - ing by,
On New Year's Day in the morn - ing.

2. And what do you think was in them then?
In them then? in them then? And what do you think was in them then,

3. Three pret - ty girls were in them then,
In them then, in them then, Three pret - ty girls were in them then,

4. And one could whis - tle, one could sing, The oth - er play on the vi - o - lin, Such joy was there at my wed - ding,
On New Year's Day in the morn - ing.

Song XXXIV

Good King Wenceslas

Song XXXV

The First Noël

Song XXXVI **Ding-Dong, Bell**

Song XXXVII **"Where are you going to, my pretty maid"?**

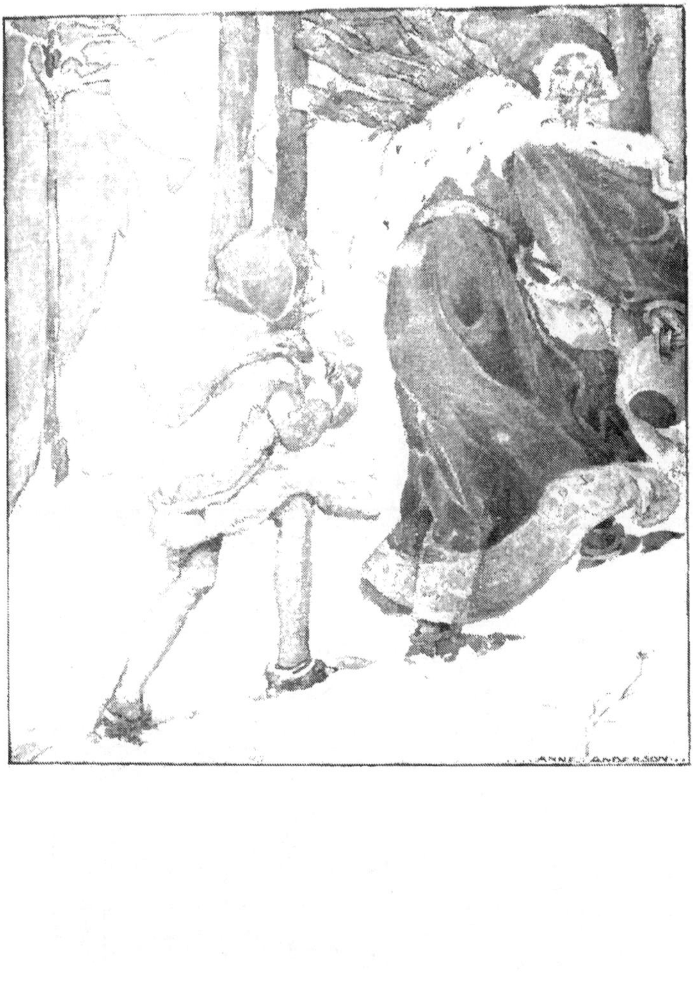
ANNE ANDERSON

Good King Wenceslas.

Quickly.

1. Good King Wen-ces-las look'd out On the feast of Step-hen, When the snow lay round a-bout, Deep and crisp and e-ven; Bright-ly shone the moon that night, Tho' the frost was cru-el, When a poor man came in sight, Gath'ring win-ter fu-el.

2. "Hi - ther page, and stand by me, If thou know'st it, tell - ing,
Yon-der pea - sant, who is he? Where and what his dwell - ing?"
"Sire, he lives a good league hence, Un-der-neath the moun-tain,
Right a-gainst the for-est fence, By Saint Ag-nes' foun - - tain."

3

' Bring me flesh, and bring me wine,
    Bring me pine-logs hither ;
Thou and I shall see him dine,
    When we bear them thither '
Page and monarch, forth they went,
    Forth they went together,
Through the rude wind's wild lament,
    And the bitter weather

4

" Sire, the night is darker now,
    And the wind blows stronger ;
Fails my heart, I know not how
    I can go no longer "
" Mark my footsteps, good my page,
    Tread thou in them boldly ;
Thou shalt find the winter's rage
    Freeze thy blood less coldly '

5

In his master's steps he trod,
    Where the snow lay dinted ;
Heat was in the very sod
    Which the saint had printed
Therefore, Christian men, be sure,
    Wealth or rank possessing,
Ye who now will bless the poor
    Shall yourselves find blessing

THE FIRST NOEL.

Moderato.

1. The first Noël the angel did say Was to certain poor shepherds in fields where they lay, In fields where they lay keeping their sheep, On a cold winter's night that was so deep.

3

And by the light of that same star
There were three wise men came from the country afar;
To seek the King it was their intent,
And to follow the star wherever it went.

    Noel, Noel, etc.

4

The star drew nigh unto the north-west,
Over Bethlehem paused, and there it did rest;
And there did shine most bright and did stay
Over where the young Child and his Mother did lay.

    Noel, Noel, etc.

5

Then entered in those wise men all three,
Very reverently, upon bended knee,
And offered there in His presence
Gifts of gold and of myrrh and of frankincense

    Noel, Noel, etc.

6

Then let us all with one accord
Sing praises unto our Heavenly Lord,
That made the heavens and earth of nought,
And with His blood mankind hath bought.

    Noel, Noel, etc.

DING-DONG-BELL

DING-DONG-BELL

drown poor lit-tle pus-sy cat, Who ne'er did an-y harm, But
Lit-tle Tom-my Stout. What a naugh-ty boy was that, To
kill'd all the mice in fa-ther's barn, in
drown poor lit-tle pus-sy cat, Who ne'er did an-y harm, But
fa-ther's barn.
kill'd all the mice in fa-ther's barn, in fa-ther's barn.

"Where are you going to, my pretty maid?"

Andante.

1. "Where are you go-ing to, my pret-ty maid?" "Where are you go-ing to, my pret-ty maid?" "I'm go-ing a-milk-ing, Sir," she said. "Sir," she said, "Sir," she said, "I'm go-ing a-milk-ing, Sir," she said.

1

" Where are you going to, my pretty maid ?
' I'm going a-milking, Sir,' she said.

2

' Shall I go with you, my pretty maid ? '
' Yes, if you please, kind Sir," she said

3

" What is your fortune, my pretty maid ? '
 My face is my fortune, Sir," she said

4

" Then I can't marry you, my pretty maid '
" Nobody asked you, Sir," she said

HERE'S A HEALTH UNTO HIS MAJESTY WITH A FA LA LA LA LADY

FINIS